The Conspiracy Quartet

THE CONSPIRACY QUARTET

DAVID CLEWELL

**Missouri Center
for the Book**

ᨃᨃᨃ

**Missouri Authors
Collection**

Garlic Press

St. Louis, Missouri

ACKNOWLEDGMENTS

Parts of this sequence have appeared in *Boulevard* ("The Accomplice"), *Poetry* ("Enough"), and *World Poetry* ("The Ground Floor" and "Frank Olson Is Flying"), an on-line publication (http://www.worldpoetry.com/). My gratitude to the editors for their early support.

ISBN 0-9643009-2-3

for Benjamin, my newest accomplice,
and Patricia, longtime loving co-conspirator
who brought him to me . . .

. . . and for Dale Woolery, informant extraordinaire,
master of the much-less-than-obvious

Never give a sucker an even break or smarten up a chump.
      —W.C. Fields, *You Can't Cheat An Honest Man*

No death for you. You are involved.
      —Weldon Kees, "The Smiles of the Bathers"

I
ENOUGH

ENOUGH

Uncle Bud would always swear *they* had a pill
you could drop into the gas tank, and miraculously
you'd be talking 200 miles to the gallon, but no, *they*
were not about to let that out, that was something
he knew for sure. He'd read it in a magazine
and it turned into one of his favorite theories,
those flimsy sticks he rubbed together
trying to light up the dark *they* worked so hard to keep him in.
Sundays we passed the mashed potatoes around the table
for their pale, watery lesson: just when we think we can't
take any more, there we are in spite of it all, helping ourselves.

Bud loved dreaming up other people's secrets, letting us know
he was onto something big this time. It put a dollop of hope
into his hapless days: *they* breathed the same planet's air
as he did, and *they* had power, cigars, prestige to burn.
The one time I actually managed to whisper *enough's enough*,
I wasn't sure who I wanted to hear it: my uncle, my mother
in the relentless bounty of her kitchen. The inexplicable blue sky.
That's what they'd *like you to believe*, he told me, *so don't.*
And right before pie I stood corrected: *You'll find out too much
is not enough, not nearly, in this life.*

Each Sunday we watched him pull away
in his dilapidated Buick, looking incredibly
smaller behind the wheel than he'd seemed the week before.
No one wanted to tell me he was dying, that cancer cells
arranged his doing-in, at first a vicious rumor
slowly spreading, then turning more insidious and true.
He had to know the pain, if not the reason. No doctors
in cahoots would ever get their hooks in him, gladly
take too many days of his hard-knock salesman's money
for x-rays and needles and biopsy slides that only
might confirm what he'd secretly been feeling all along:
There's nothing we can do.

And I remember thinking:
if there truly is a pill, it would be only fair
to let him have it, finally, no questions asked. How much
could it hurt? And he wouldn't have to stop and ask
directions he never quite trusted. Or resign himself
to another three dollars of Regular and hope
he wouldn't run out before he made it halfway to anywhere.
In theory just this once he could drive himself crazy
or elated, unbelievably whole, and keep on going,
humming along with the steady engine—a secret at last
sized so exactly to his heart's desire that maybe he'd find himself
feeling like one of *them* for a minute, and for a minute more
at least, that would be enough. And having gone as far as he could—
almost off the map, falling into blue—maybe then
he'd really pull over, kick off his dependable shoes,
all in due time, forever.
                              And I knew it wouldn't be Uncle Bud
without one of the bad habits he couldn't break, swearing
his luck had changed into something more comfortable and good.
So I imagined him spitting into the ocean, still intent
on making his small difference, even in the face
of his own ridiculous dying: waiting out the dark, the rising tide,
staking every one of his feverish claims all over again in the sand
at the edge of the knowable world.

II
Smithereens: Roswell, New Mexico

i. Pieces of a Story

Some stories practically tell themselves—short
and straightforward, believe them or not:
when private pilot Kenneth Arnold described the nine objects
he'd spotted near Mt. Ranier, Washington, on June 24, 1947,
he said they moved like saucers skipping across a lake. The End.
In one breath Arnold gave *flying saucers* to post-war America
and, for a while, the entire world was looking up.

But two weeks later the bottom dropped out when something big
suddenly came apart in the sky, scattering debris
over nearly a mile of the Foster sheep ranch outside Roswell.
Foreman Mac Brazel wasn't thinking *flying saucer*
when he gathered up some of those featherweight pieces of metal.
But no matter the surely more reasonable, down-to-earth
explanation, he was still certain this fell outside
the range of his cowboy expertise. A few days later
he let the local sheriff talk him into bringing
whatever he'd found to the Roswell Army Air Field.

Mac didn't think he had much of a story. No,
he hadn't seen anything go down. Maybe
he'd heard an explosion during a thunderstorm, but
that was one more detail he couldn't swear to.
He showed the officers how easily they could manipulate
the silvery material, although no one could break
even the flimsiest-looking piece. He watched them try
to burn it, tear it, scratch it, dent it
with a sixteen-pound sledge. The oddball metal returned
to its original shape every time. Someone called it
the damnedest thing. Mac just wanted to know
when they'd get around to clearing it off his land.

Two Army investigators headed back with Brazel
to see the actual wreckage for themselves.

They loaded what they could into a '42 Buick convertible,
into a sizable jeep. When Major Jesse Marcel stopped home
on his way back to the base, he couldn't believe
what he was about to show his family, fast,
before his story was *Classified*. They spread out the pieces
on the kitchen floor and did what everyone else would be doing
for years: tried somehow to fit them together.
They tried to make sense of the tiny hieroglyphics
his son pointed out in a certain slant of light.
For the next three decades Marcel would keep quiet,
his professional oath of uneasy silence. But he would swear,
surrounded by his family, it was *nothing from this Earth*.

The next morning *The Roswell Daily Record* had its story,
straight from an overzealous public-information officer:
RAAF CAPTURES FLYING SAUCER ON RANCH IN ROSWELL REGION.
But by the later edition, that story had fallen apart,
changed shape completely: nothing but a downed weather balloon.
There's a sheepish Marcel on his knees in a general's office,
holding up a few telltale scraps for the cameras.
And the military looked upon its own creation and saw that it was
pretty good, for a rush job.

And this became the determined story
of The Little Weather Balloon That Couldn't—good enough,
apparently, to entertain officers flying in from installations
all over the country. Good enough to detain Mac Brazel
at the Roswell base for a week.
                              Meanwhile, back at the ranch,
the Army declared a Restricted Area: riflemen in the hills,
MPs manning roadblocks. Troops sweeping for radiation,
engaged in a two-day clean-up of the hundreds of shards still left.
They were told *maybe a V-2 rocket* gone awry, maybe
something more sinister, *possibly Russian*. Or maybe this:
what Ken Arnold gave over to a slaphappy nation,

the military took away *in the interests of national security*. The End,
okay? Now: lights out, eyes closed,
sweet dreams. And no peeking, in the interests of
national insecurity, once upon a time in Roswell.

And when Mac's released, he's never heard of
any flying disc. He's given someone his word in exchange
for a spiffy new pick-up, a house in a wealthier county.
And suddenly he's as boring as the next guy. The weather's
all he can talk about. Sure, he'd made them pay, but the brass
was getting off cheap: as far as they could tell, he didn't know
anything about three bodies near the crash site—although
there were nights he woke up excited in the middle of
his wildest dreams, already forgetting untold pieces.

Someone should have struck a deal with Glenn Dennis too,
the Roswell mortician who would never forget
the barrage of phone calls from the base in a single afternoon:
what will this chemical do to blood? What will that one do
to the tissue? And how would someone try making up bodies
that have been out in the sun for a week?

They could have come through with something for Oliver "Pappy"
Henderson, who flew the C-54 without lights
to Ohio's Wright Field. Sooner or later he'd wonder out loud
why MPs were assigned to the crate he was carrying
in the unpressurized belly of his plane.

And why no keys to a Buick convertible for Norma Gardner, typist
with top security at Wright? By the time this story gets to her,
she's preparing two unheard-of autopsy reports. No, they weren't
ready for a third one quite yet. They still weren't ready
twelve years later, when Norma retired, letting it slip
out the door with her into the civilian air: someone
might be saving the best part of the Roswell story
for last.

17

So many people to take at their word, and even
at that, there may be less mystery, more prosaic explanations.
We're always so sure of ourselves, convinced we'll know
the real story when we hear it. But truth is, sometimes
it's not that easy to tell:

ii. The Airships of Aurora

Out of the nineteenth-century blue, from November 1896 to May 1897: thousands of people across America reported witnessing what they could only call an *airship* cruising overhead. In Sacramento, Omaha, Chicago, they rushed into the streets or climbed up to rooftops to get a glimpse. One newspaper reported a new malady, *airship neck*, resulting from people's unbelievable efforts to see it.

By century's end, this was a nation drunk on progress and hopelessly in love with invention. Thomas Edison was the quintessential American hero. Almost anything seemed technically possible.

And the fledgling science fiction so popular in the '80s and '90s already had invented the airship. In Jules Verne's *Robur the Conqueror*, serialized in American newspapers as *Clipper of the Clouds*, Robur is a Captain Nemo–like genius who attempts to conquer the world with his incredible airship. But there's also astounding American teenager Luis Seranens and his extraordinarily popular "Frank Reade Invention Novel Series," from which a by-now-tired-of-prognosticating Verne lifted the airship idea. *Frank Reade and His Airship . . . Frank Reade in the Clouds . . . Frank Reade with His Airship in Africa*—novels that ran in the weekly pulps, later reprinted in the Wide Awake Library: all published before *Robur*. Only an infinitesimal portion of Seranens' forty million words, written in longhand. No one can invent characters like that anymore.

The primary means of faster-than-longhand, long-distance communication was the railroad telegraph, which spread the airship hysteria. A telegraph operator in Iowa tried to confess: he'd started it all by stitching together the tallest tale he could think of out of thin air. But he was shouted down, drowned out by hundreds of newspapers thinking only of circulation.

In addition to reporting the latest accounts, papers across the country carried even more exotic renditions: meetings with the crew. Trips aboard the craft at 100 mph. Interviews with a mysterious inventor—always a crackpot genius, evil or otherwise—who'd secretly perfected his vessel in his hidden desert laboratory. Editorials about high-society life on other planets. A melodramatic abduction or two.

And the men of science moved in for the kill, debunking every manifestation of this lighter-than-air business.

The Wright Brothers and Kitty Hawk were still seven years in the future. Even then, we're talking a rickety, twelve-second flight. The dirigible—a rigid, steerable balloon—was further along in development in 1896, but still: at that point, it had too long a way to go. There's no doubt: people had been soaring for over a century, but in no particular direction; the Montgolfier Brothers launched the first manned balloon flight in 1783. From there, the entire idea of human flight was up in the air.

The Dallas Morning News was taking the national airship frenzy as a joke. They interviewed an eyewitness in nearby Farmersville who reported *three men in an airship singing 'Nearer, My God to Thee' while distributing temperance tracts.*

By the summer of 1897, the sightings dropped off. The sky was vast and empty again. Newspaper coverage stopped almost completely. From something that caused such ubiquitous buzzing, the airship turned into a subject no one talked about—deliberately forgotten, it seemed, even by those who'd experienced it. Its sudden plunge into oblivion is a mystery almost as great as its appearance in the first place.

• • • •

On April 17, 1897, the good citizens of Aurora, Texas watched an airship flying north over their town, at times travelling so close to the ground that observers thought it had to be experiencing mechanical difficulty. *The Dallas Morning News*, fifty miles south, saw it this way:

> *It sailed gradually over the public square and, when it reached the north part of town, collided with the tower of Judge Proctor's windmill and went to pieces with a terrific explosion, scattering debris over several acres of ground, wrecking the windmill and destroying the judge's flower garden.*

The windmill, at least, was a reporter's invention; there was no such contraption anywhere near the Proctor place. But the bloom wasn't quite off the rose: searchers supposedly found *the badly disfigured body of a being* that one T.J. Weems, *a U.S. Signal Service officer and authority on astronomy*, declared to be *a native of the planet Mars*.

Weems was Aurora's hardworking town blacksmith, an authority on horses. And try as he might, he couldn't even pick out Pegasus in a given night's scattering of stars.

The 1890s saw increasing support for the theory that Mars was crisscrossed by a planet-spanning network of artificial canals. This presumed the existence of actual Martians to dig them. Percival Lowell, one of the nation's leading astronomers, actively advanced the idea, founding an observatory in the Arizona desert—where he thought he could see things more clearly—in an effort to prove his belief. His conception—of a civilization engaged in a battle for survival with a dying planet by diverting water from the polar caps to the more desiccated equatorial regions—caught the public imagination like nothing else in the science of the period.

And this wasn't offered as science fiction: not overworked Verne, or even prodigious pulpmeister Seranens. Civil War Confederate soldier John Carter had left his own starlit Arizona landscape (. . . *enchanting and inspiring, so different from the aspect of any other spot upon our Earth . . . it's as though one were catching for the first time a glimpse of some dead and forgotten world*) for the planet Mars (*I closed my eyes, stretched out my arms toward the god of my vocation, and felt myself drawn with the suddenness of thought through the trackless immensity of space*) and returned by then. But Edgar Rice Burroughs telling the world about it was another fifteen years away.

This was Percival Lowell, of the Boston Lowells, of the Lowells-talk-only-to-the-Cabots-and-the-Cabots-talk-only-to-God.

It took seventy years to completely kill off that version of valiant Martians, when a series of unmanned Mariner probes took fly-by close-up pictures. The canals had been a tantalizing optical illusion: the combination of random topographical Martian detail and the innately human tendency to try organizing such detail into a meaningful pattern.

Papers found on the pilot's person—evidently the records of his travels—are written in some unknown hieroglyphics and cannot be deciphered. The ship was too badly wrecked to form any conclusion as to its construction or motive power. It was built of an unknown metal, resembling somewhat a mixture of aluminum and silver. The town today is full of people who are viewing the wreckage and gathering specimens of the strange metal from the debris. The pilot's funeral will take place at noon tomorrow.

There was no follow-up story. No high-noon Texas drama. The entire affair was laid to rest in the boondocks of wishful thinking.

• • • •

On the outskirts of Aurora, under a limb of the oldest
gnarled oak in the cemetery, there is a peculiar
circular grave. Until 1973, it was marked
by a triangular headstone, into which a crude image
of a cigar-shaped object was chiselled. Or maybe
not. Maybe it was a natural indentation
in the impressionable stone. Or some kind of accident—
say, the careless bite of a plow blade.
The stone was stolen in the dead of a summer night:
dug up, lifted, carried clean away.

                                        Every few years since,
someone blows in from out of town to dig through
Aurora's municipal records, looking for substantiation:
a sensational story buried in the small print
of a hundred years. Filing requests to unearth a miracle
or fabrication—whatever might be found out there.
The three hundred citizens, who can't remember hearing
anything special about 1897, have managed to ward off
exhumation every time. It's become a massive undertaking,
this looking after their own small-town dead. No one
has any tales—tall or otherwise—left to tell.

After the theft, Aurora hired security for the graveyard:
a retired preacher with his own shotgun. Personally,
he'd rather believe in something than in nothing, but he can't
believe what he's seen: *When the railroad passed us by,*
the whole town started dying. We were the county seat,
3,000 strong. That airship thing was supposed to carry us
into the twentieth century. But look around.

                                        He can't believe
some people's cockeyed faith. He's had about all he can take
of the twentieth century: *You want Martians? Go to Roswell.*
We're fresh out of 'em here.

iii. Back on the Map, Not Far from Wherever You Are

Roswell got lost for decades in the flying saucer deluge. The few who were talking back then were drowned out by those reliably goofy 1950s contactees—self-styled conduits of unearthly, harmonious wisdom they gathered from the saucerfolk light-years ahead of us intellectually, emotionally, spiritually, technologically—and who suddenly seemed compelled to land here just long enough to let us know it. From whatever desert, woods, or clearing on the fringe of their boardinghouse days and nights, our contactees hitched jaunty rides to other planets, other stars, any place they imagined capable of supporting the rest of their lives.

And they came back talking it up, writing it down in books, in pamphlets, in plastic spiral binders. Years beyond Orson Welles and his invasion of the airwaves by malevolent Martians, there wasn't much Mars in their madness. Everything was coming up Venus, where things were cloudier, cooler, more capable of sustaining love:

George Adamski, short-order cook with his homemade telescope in the shadow of Mt. Palomar, became the movement's senior statesman. He settled for touring the United States and Europe when his more far-flung wanderings ended. George Van Tassel, who came back to Earth and sponsored the annual Giant Rock, California conventions for fellow off-the-map travellers. Howard Menger, New Jersey sign painter–turned–inventor-of-anti-gravity–devices, in UPI photos side by side with his Saturnian bride (they *met* on Venus), who looked like any other North Jersey Connie, Arlene, or Estelle. Buck Nelson actually sold the actual hair of the Venusian dog that bit him. His biggest surprise, if not ours: the Venusians were wearing overalls exactly like his.

And the aliens they confabulated with never once seemed to crash and burn. They knew their way around a solar system. They knew the art of the soft landing. They always made a point of taking off after handing over their inscrutable pieces of Universal Understanding.

But Roswell came before those benevolent Space Brothers—and the occasional shimmering Space Sister—had anything to say to the credulous likes of us.

Before any of the officially serious Air Force investigations of what would soon be more politely known as Unidentified Flying Objects: Project *Sign*. The aptly named Project *Grudge*. Their longest—and last: Project *Blue Book*. Not finding much of anything, they're officially out of the UFO business in 1969.

Before Gabriel Green, president of the Amalgamated Flying Saucer Clubs of America and his run for the presidency of the United States on his bumper-sticker platform: *FLYING SAUCERS ARE REAL—IT'S THE AIR FORCE THAT DOESN'T EXIST*. He lost overwhelmingly to JFK, and three years later felt strangely complicit, calling a press conference where he assumed that somehow *the Interplanetarians were in on that Dallas thing*.

Before the infamous *swamp gas* explanation of a mystery, there was Roswell.

Before hypnosis led us as a country to believe that over five million of our own had been abducted by aliens obsessed with mostly invasive implantations, and you can forget all about your Universal Understanding. You can stick that up some galaxy where the sun doesn't shine.

Before any New Age channelling of alien intelligences like Ashtar, Mars Sector 6, or Uriel—who all sound like any high school Tiffany or Brent—by a few of us who wanted in on the tenuous wisdom or were simply that desperate for any company at all, but were too afraid to literally get onboard and fly.

• • • •

We've found Roswell again. We've heard it from someone
who got it from someone else who knows
a person that some of the hush-hushing really happened to.
Across time and space, the Roswell machinery is up
and flying again—the UFO equivalent of The Mouse
in the Coke, The Hook, The Phantom Hitchhiker. And if alleged
eyewitnesses are dying, it's no cabal of systematic elimination.
It's no coincidence, either: 1947 is everyone's mostly
better part of a lifetime ago.

Sleepy Roswell's back
on the national map, re-zoned, a metropolis of possibilities.
It's turned into a paranoid pop culture mantra, a word
intoned to stand in for Whatever Happened There in movies,
weekly TV spook shows, and supermarket checkout racks.
There's even a comic book series called *Roswell*, in this case
the name of the spunky, surviving alien who lives
for his share of adventures with a beautiful Earthling inventor,
barely fazed in the least by the military's predictable,
misguided efforts to reclaim him.
This cartoon alien looks a lot
like Buckey Bug, pre-Roswell 1930s Disney Studios bit player
who never quite hit the big time, prone as he was to speaking
in verse. But there doesn't seem to be much easy poetry in Roswell.

• • • •

Alien t-shirts, neckties, and boxers are hawked at the mall.
Alien-head coffee mugs, necklaces. Alien candelabra. Adopt your own
Alien-in-Formaldehyde, complete with Biohazard Container.
(*Fill jar 3/4 full of water . . . add a drop or two of food color.*
To keep alien upright, use a drop of Super Glue on alien's bottom
and position it before adding water.) A rancher in Roswell
will sell you soil *from on or near the crash site.*
He pours it into the plastic dome of the cheapest flying saucer
on Earth and sends along a personal Certificate of Authenticity.

Take your choice of alien abduction support groups. Alien lollipops
that glow in the dark. Aliens in cereal commercials,
camera promotions, insurance ads for comprehensive life.
The brothers doing a brisk business in *Roswell or Bust!*
hitchhiking alien dolls at the flea market have a theory:
the government as ultimate wholesaler, softening us up,
preparing us to hear one more Official Truth: the undeniable
presence of some kind of intelligent life here on Earth.
They should only know that we want in, A.S.A.P.,
that we'd be willing to settle for any kind of dirt on
or near Anything That Important—certifiable or not.
No one expects even homemade guarantees. We're puny
Earthlings, reinventing ourselves each day, but we're still
no match for the likes of Roswell. It's all we can do
to follow the bygone adventures of Buckey Bug:

• • • •

Buckey Bug had always yearned to see the world. He was a very little fellow, but that did not deter him from his purpose of seeking adventure. So he built himself a stout little boat from a walnut shell and rigged up a nice limber oak leaf for a sail. . . .

Buckey sailed on and on until he lost all track of time and distance. He passed away the hours in cheerful song and contemplation of the future. But all the while, disaster lurked in the air. . . . The wind rose to a mighty tempest that lashed the sea into a seething fury. And Buckey's little ship was tossed about like straw. When the storm had subsided, his little craft was cast high and dry upon a reef along the coast of a strange land.

Buckey survives, of course. He's one plucky bug. It must be the poet in him:

> *Some time ago I left my home,*
> *deciding that I ought to roam*
> *and hunt for fortune and for fame,*
> *and bring some glory to my name!*
> *And now that some success I've had,*
> *I'm going back to Mom and Dad.*

A pithy recapitulation in iambic tetrameter. In nearly heroic couplets. And along with the rest of the civilized world, the Air Force couldn't care less.

• • • •

Regardless of the aliens' original objectives,
they've become just so much merchandise, the Troll Dolls
of the '90s. We've packaged yet another phenomenon
we don't really understand, made it safe for human consumption.

And for true enthusiasts, Roswell's nearly passé—sensational
in its time, but already yesterday's news. Around the electric fires
of photocopiers, faxes, and e-mail transmissions, people gather
to catch the latest edition of Roswell's shadowy, ghost-story
sequel: Groom Lake, Nevada. Area 51.
It's as if everyone's in some mainstream approximation of The Know:
the elaborate, subterranean layout. The absolutely
outrageous deal cut decades ago with the captured aliens
(is there anyone left who doesn't know them as *the Greys*?):
human subjects for their insidious genetic experimentation
in exchange for the impenetrable secrets of their flying machines.

(And just wait until the mainstream catches up with
tomorrow's news: Operation D-6. Dulce, New Mexico. Now *there's*
an underground wonderment, a hybrid arrangement you wouldn't believe.
But that's another story. And so far it's not for sale.)

These days it's doubtful any Greys still inhabit the premises.
It's the '90s. With cell phones, our troubleshooters from the stars
are always within reach. Now it's only the Air Force
still working out the bugs. This is nuts-and-bolts hardware
at its aerodynamic best. A story light-years in the making,
but they finally got the impossible off the ground.

There are stunning satellite photos of this base that officially
doesn't exist. And isn't called The Box or The Ranch
or The Funny Farm by the hundreds of *Priority Clearance* engineers
who aren't flown in weekly from all around the nation.
No wonder the sky out there is lit up all the time.

No wonder the generals drink a bit. The whole thing's
one big, bad Dreamland, no more or less
fantastical than any other governmental tossing and turning:
trafficking opium in Southeast Asia. Trading arms to Iran
for American hostages. Those exploding cigars for Castro.
No wonder there's no way of guessing what in the world
they'll be dreaming up in the long nights ahead.

At Groom Lake the skittish lights in the sky,
no matter what they really are, belong to us.
At least we've come that far. It's hard to believe,
but this might be the only place in the country without
a single alien in sight. All the Space Brothers have been here
and gone, trying to tell us, in so many words: the most
unlikely maneuvers in the dark have always been our own.

iv. Interlude: As Frolicsome As It Gets

And in the town of Roswell, they've always known
a good thing when they see it. Not one,
but two museums devoted to the crash and fifty years
of attendant hoopla. On anniversary weekends
there's a parade down Main Street. Folks dress up
like the almond-eyed aliens, or deck themselves out
like the military—or it *is* the military, taking notes.
The local high school band plays spirited,
corny versions of all the appropriate tunes: *Great Balls
of Fire*. Sheb Wooley's *Flying Purple People Eater*.
And their signature finale, *Wipe-Out*.
Right behind them there's a Crashed Saucer float
made of chicken wire, flashlights, and aluminum foil.

At this rate, there's not a lot of room
for skeptics in the street: one kid in serious glasses
at the tail end of the spectacle, buzzing away
on Buddy Holly's *That'll Be the Day*. But even at that,
it's a flying saucer kazoo. He's too young to believe
that no one's listening, that he might as well save his breath.

v. The Revised Adventures of Ballooning

In its 1994 report on the Roswell incident, the Air Force finally and officially admitted that 1947's weather balloon explanation had been a cover story. And in that much-published photo of Jesse Marcel kneeling on the floor in his general's office, Marcel suddenly looks less sheepish, more clearly pissed. Insisting, at the corners of his mouth, this isn't at all what fell out of the sky. They'd handed him the role of scapegoat—*inexperienced field investigator*— and for thirty years he took it, for the sake of his career and, more vaguely, his country. But mainly he had his family to think of, and they knew from the beginning that what he was holding onto for the cameras was a lie—or at least the first of a few "revisions."

The 1994 Air Force version: okay, not a weather balloon, but a piece of Project *Mogul*—Top Secret, high-altitude balloons designed to detect Soviet nuclear weapon explosions in the upper atmosphere. Early Cold War shenanigans that still had nothing to do with any invasion from outer space, they promised.

There really *was* a Project *Mogul*. There really was a Russia. And there really, really was a whole lot of shaking going on in New Mexico, for all of its open spaces. Manhattan had come to the desert: Los Alamos, the new atomic nerve center. White Sands Proving Grounds. The Trinity test site near Alamagordo: a yellow glow; a white, blinding flash; then the first mushroom cloud in history blowing up out of a nowhere July 16, 1945 New Mexico morning. And the *Enola Gay* flew out of Roswell's 509th Bomb Group three weeks later with *Little Boy* in its belly—four tons of atomic bomb that would go to pieces over Hiroshima.

And in 1995, the one thousand pages of summaries, diagrams, and documents published by the U.S. Government Printing Office—more *Mogul* than ever we needed to know—*The Roswell Report: Fact vs. Fiction in the New Mexico Desert*. A viable subtitle, no matter what side of the Roswell story we eventually happen to come down on.

Here's one more revision: an Even More Top Secret herd of gigantic balloon animals some government clowns were testing, twisting the truth about Roswell until it turned into a cow, a donkey, a horse's ass. Launching them into the vastness of space that has always been over our heads. And waiting— for decades, if necessary—to see if ordinary civilians can tell the truth, when they see it, from so much hot air. And what they might possibly do if it explodes in their unsuspecting faces.

vi. Home Movies of the Dead

The theories, opinions, and beliefs expressed are not the only possible
interpretation.

A universal disclaimer. From time to time, depending
where we've put our faith on any given day, we need reminding.
When we're face to face with the bank teller, the landlord,
or the belly dancer, let's consider ourselves forewarned.
And when it crawls across the screen just before the Alien
Autopsy footage and subsequent partisan "analysis,"
it's virtually a guarantee:

Two guys in contamination suits taking apart what we're asked to see as the
body of an extraterrestrial. It seems too large, even for the Roswell folklore—
one extra digit on each hand and foot instead of the gospel reports of one less.
Injuries don't look extensive enough, given the solemn recitations of the
crash's magnitude. And the bleeding is too easy, too extravagantly human.
There's no irrefutable evidence, nothing in-our-face that says *Roswell*. But
these days, when it comes to dead aliens, Roswell's all we know. Roswell's
the living end.

The movie's black-and-white, jumpy, in and out of focus, like a lot of America
after the war. There's no script, no soundtrack, no words at all to describe
what's going on. In their living rooms doubters and believers alike improvise
the same line and repeat it until they've got their parts down, cold: *This can't
really be happening.*

According to the straight face of the authentic 1940s clock on the wall, the
procedure takes just a couple of hours. It's the autopsy of a lifetime, and these
guys are working as if they're afraid of missing the meat loaf plate at lunch.
The telephone, the surgical instruments, the contamination gear all appear to
be actual 1947 possibilities. So we have to concede the tiniest chance that this
scene may not have been staged and more recently shot, trying for some fifty-
years-ago verisimilitude.

And what's there on the table depends, as always, on what we bring to it, on which road to some semblance of the facts we're trying to negotiate: a being from a completely different world of genetic disorders or radiation victims. Of Hollywood special effects or far-fetched, long-travelling carbon-based life forms. No matter what conclusion we finally draw, there's bound to be something wrong with this picture.

In the Alien Autopsy industry, rumor has it that the photographer who shot the footage is still alive and wants no part of the worldwide publicity. Like the last crash-surviving alien himself, he's said to be in different places: Florida. Arizona. A rooming house in New York City. The supposedly modest money he made was supposedly for his granddaughter. British music distributor Ray Santilli was buying our shy cameraman's film of Elvis-in-the-Army when he was offered this other alien body as well—twenty-two cannisters of unprocessed astonishment that, if you can believe it, the military never bothered asking for in over forty years.

This sale went down right around the time the Air Force was doing some selling of its own, releasing its Project *Mogul* findings—a black-and-white explanation if ever there was one—and wondering who would buy it.

Nearly a generation after *Don't Be Cruel*, Elvis had taken to wearing other-worldly jumpsuits. He seemed too big, even for the rock 'n' roll folklore. But he was still wowing the crowds. One of his last huge hits: *Suspicious Minds*.

———————

Elvis or the cameraman or the third surviving alien,
whose trio was briefly at the top of the charts, at the top
of the goddamn world: we need someone to come forward.
We want something larger than a day to put our faith in,
hard. And if we find anything that can be interpreted
only one way, it's possible we could end up
wearing it thin, believing it to death.

vii. Something's Always Going Down

If this is the mystery it's cracked up to be, then we're missing
the requisite bodies. In typical whodunnits, they're found
larger than life on someone's drawing-room floor. And they stay
in one place long enough for death to sink in. Finally it's time
for the clever detective to make his living, working backwards
through the most likely facts until he finds out the one person
no one else would have guessed. He understands the process,
the tedious arithmetic of elimination.

But this is a different story, a nearly existential mystery
that begins with naming the usual suspects, then deciding what
they possibly could have done. Someone's always looking forward
to those witnesses with their spectacular claims: *You-Know-Who*
did *Who-Knows-What*, they're positive of that much.
Every day's more living proof, if only we could see it
their way. And no one anywhere on the planet finally
has a story so convincing that it puts them far enough away
from the scene of every imaginable crime.
This is about the dizzying process of making things add up
before they get taken away. This is about trying to fit together
too many dubious pieces in the imagination's hot kitchen.
But as so often is the case: no evidence
is hard enough. It's the gossamer of circumstance.
And the trail is half-a-century cold.

Someone once must have had the slightest clue,
quietly must have chosen never to give up
what he was holding onto: just one unassuming shred of the wreck
the whole town picked up on when the story first exploded.
One keepsake retrieved on the fly, secreted away
for posterity, whatever it might turn out to be. Maybe
in a shoebox, a suitcase, a bus station locker. At the bottom
of a neighbor girl's hope chest. He'd hold out just that much
forever, in a place he was sure no one would think of—or at least
as far as he could tell: the rest of his uneventful life.

And despite the official hush-hush, *Eyes Only* designation,
there should have been someone with a camera
who couldn't resist: two or three secret souvenir pictures
of those well-travelled bodies themselves, somewhere
in clandestine transit. Unauthorized, snapped in a hurry, now lost
in the blur of their own safekeeping: say, too many innocuous years
of Family Summer Vacation albums. Wherever they are, they can't be
entirely out of the question yet, but they're undeniably fading
after all this time in light of the unlikely story
someone's still counting on them for. Right after the pages
of Tillie and Gus at Yellowstone (*We were so happy then. . . .*)
and Aunt Ida on horseback (*Having a wonderful time. . . .*):
the aliens preserved in formaldehyde. Wish they were here.

An honestly dramatic deathbed confession would be nice:
They're underground in Nevada or *on ice at Wright Field* or
in my goddamn basement. Believe it or not. And then
exactly the right number of details, instead of the usual
too few or too many. This is the Crashed Saucer Story
everyone wants a piece of, dusted off after decades of neglect,
remodeled for our more unabashedly conspiratorial times.
And why not, in a world where we don't ever want to be
at a loss to explain anything from the vagaries of physics
to the blown tires of love, our uneasiness at breakfast
and the shadows we cast, shrinking up to nothing
in the glare of the noonday sun.

• • • •

In the name of research you might even get in the car
and drive out to Roswell, to Corona, to the desolate Plains
of San Agustin: a completely different planet.
You might really think—despite the years that have flown by
and no matter how many people have covered the same ground—
you've made it this far for a reason, an explanation if only
you could find the one piece everyone else somehow left behind.
If you presumed anything less, you wouldn't be out there,
wouldn't be human, looking up against the incredible odds
for something falling from the sky one more time: some crazy
resilient answer you've been waiting for amid the smithereens
of a lifetime, the psychic wreckage of another day
you felt yourself suddenly going to pieces. Irretrievably alone.

You still have no earthly idea what went down in 1947,
but you can feel it in the air: something's always going down
where you can't see it. It's too impossible to suppose
otherwise. Eventually by accident you're bound to be there
at some new collusion's Ground Zero, unbelievably in The Know
from the very start. On the other side of the questions for once
where now the only thing left for you to do is live long enough
to get it right, your rendition of exactly what happened.

And when they come with their attachés and their badges
to take that away from you, maybe you'll know better
how to do what you absolutely have to do again:
how to pick up even the most intangible pieces remaining
on the trail of the same old story: making it alive
through one more version of a day you can't begin
to answer for, if only you can find it in yourself. Or wherever
in the world, from out of whatever blue that last one came,
so unmistakably promising, to you.

III
CIA IN WONDERLAND

And ye shall know the Truth and the Truth shall set you free.
    —Biblical inscription on the wall of the main lobby at CIA
    Headquarters, Langley, Virginia

i. The Ground Floor

This is before guru Leary, before the Fillmores
East and West. Before Harvard or Millbrook, acid's own
private academy. Before the Pranksters ever
set foot on the bus. Before Lucy in the Sky or the hundreds
of raucous tabloid headlines like GIRL, 5, EATS LSD
AND GOES ON RAMPAGE. Before Flower Power took
to the streets. Before Human Be-Ins. Before the Haight.

This is 1949, and the CIA is already going wild
just thinking about LSD; there are memos full of *the secret
that's going to unlock the Universe*. They're looking
for a key, let's give them that. But the Universe might be
a little much for them right now. This is about who knows
how many secrets. This is about choosing sides: someone's
got a Cold War to win. This much, finally, is about how
The Company works: a few human beings in the paranoia business
can accomplish more than any outright politics of hate.

And this leads to the clandestine 1950s birth of MK-ULTRA,
a secret-within-a-secret, the CIA's special hush-hush baby
cutting its crooked teeth on the best of everything
its cloak-and-dagger daddy can buy. These are the days
of chemical and biological abracadabra, and there must be
some magic they can do with this amazing stuff from Sandoz,
now that they've contracted for exclusive buying rights.
And so the CIA scientists get cracking.

They're not in this
for the glory, for the sacrament, for the fleeting glimpse
into altered states of being. Russia's already one reality
too many, so they're testing what they've been made to believe
could be a weapon, if only they can find a reliable trigger.
They're studying pharmaceutical ballistics, making it up
as they go along, diagramming theoretically spectacular

trick shots *sure to break the will of enemy agents*:
the soundtrack from a cartoon training film playing over
and over in some projection room above them.

And the hell with any mystical doors of perception. Show them
a window of opportunity instead, no matter how fogged-up:
If LSD proves to be inefficacious as a truth drug,
we will consider its potential as anti-interrogation substance.
Under its spell, our agents might be impervious to questioning.
Pop a tab of acid while in the fabled *enemy hands*, and suddenly
it's a different cartoon: that's Tweety, wide-eyed in the dark
of Sylvester's furry clutches: *I tawt I taw a puddy tat!*

This research gets a lot sillier, a whole lot
scarier later on. For now it's still about exhilaration:
I did! I did taw a puddy tat! Or words to that effect:
One small suitcase full of LSD could unstring every man,
woman, and child in America. Either way, there's no denying
the sheer adrenaline surge that always comes with knowing
just enough to be dangerous. They can't seem to understand
what manner of beast they're swinging around by the tail.
They'd love to let go about now and walk away with their lives,
but we can see the obvious problem: they're already in
way over their cartoon heads, so far there's nothing
totally out of the question. Nothing they won't think of next.

ii. Physician, Heal Thyself . . . But Barber, Don't Try Cutting Your Own Hair

At first the CIA was interested only in willing participation. It was a decision with more swagger than humility in it: they would prepare for operational testing by taking the LSD themselves. And maybe it seemed like a good idea at the time: government agents on drugs they'd barely had a chance to imagine.

For weeks they took turns stirring it into their morning coffee. They tripped at the office, in the streets, at home. They fired off memos and service revolvers, drove spiffy convertibles, went shopping for ties. They ran zigzag on the beach and made whatever love they had left at the end of the day.

Sometimes they worked in pairs, and it was high school gym class all over again: one person somewhere on the ropes. The other person playing spotter, trying to look busy, hoping the coach will forget they're supposed to trade places when his partner comes down.

They observed, questioned, analyzed each other. They put in for overtime to make sense of their copious notes. By now the reasoning was monotonously simple: if they could *penetrate the Inner Self* and reach some kind of tenuous understanding, they would *know better how to manipulate a person—or how to keep him from being manipulated.*

One is known by The Company one keeps.

There were unmitigated disasters. But a few surprising triumphs, too. And which was which depended a lot on who was doing the talking.

• • • •

What came through the closed door was the realization . . . the direct, total awareness, from the inside . . . of Love as the primary and fundamental cosmic fact.
— Aldous Huxley, describing his first LSD experience

I didn't want to leave it. I felt I would be going back to a place where I wouldn't be able to hold onto this kind of beauty. . . . The people who wrote the report on me said I had experienced depression, but they didn't understand why I felt so bad. They thought I had had a bad trip.
— CIA operative, on his own LSD experience

For me it seemed as if the sky itself was opening up, and every bit
of available light from whatever passes these close-fisted days for
heaven came pouring down. In no time I found myself made up entirely
of all the colors in the visible spectrum. I was Agent ROY G. BIV,
a grade school mnemonic come to life in the street, where everything
became its own rainbow, layer after layer of light so soft I was sure
nothing on Earth would ever break again. Sharp edges disappeared
in a flash, and people's hearts fluttered out of their cages,
flying through that Monet afternoon: faces of the picnickers,
cherry blossoms falling, the bridges over the grey Potomac
all suspended an eternity together in mid-air, in molecule
after woozy molecule of Monet's definition of light. This world
so suddenly absorbing whispered its first secret in my ear:
it existed side by side with the one I was outgrowing, a cheap
seersucker suit and white bucks I never wanted to be caught dead in.

And I was in love all over the place: with the woman in the bakery,
shimmering among the cruellers in her powdered sugar coat of light.
With the blind man working the newsstand, with his light touch,
with feeling he could somehow see exactly what I was seeing: yes,
we were surrounded by light, but we were also part of the light
around everything else: the ecstatic hum of morning traffic,
shopkeepers lowering their awnings, another day's auspicious signs.

I could have kissed the glowing head of Ike himself, but then
there would have been Nixon, waiting for his. And there's no light
in Nixon: black-and-white exception, hallucination without end. And still

I must have walked a dozen miles in convoluted love until I came to
a sad understanding: all this was bound to wear off completely, fade
like even the finest perfume and the woman who swore it would last
forever in the middle of someone's wildest dream.
I didn't want to turn the sorry corner where things would be colored
only one way or another for the rest of my official life:
briefings, contacts, passports, false I.D., a wife who's not allowed
to know me half as well as she might think: this year I'm in sales
and I have to travel. Believe me, there's no pleasure in explaining
every trip I take these days is someone else's business.

———————

Today another agent took his turn. It's a joke around the office
coffee pot: *What would you like in that?* Just the thought of coffee
was enough to make him nervous, but he took the steaming cup from me
as if it were a ceremonial torch. Later he ran out of here like a man
on fire, and given his weeping and yelling, I'd have to say love
was the furthest thing from his mind. It was the only way he could tell
his side of the beguiling LSD story. I finally found him broken down,
trembling in a downtown fountain. He'd barely begun, and already
his face was washed-out, the moon reflected in water. In nothing flat
his code name was *Apple* to my *Orange*, our sadnesses that incomparable.

But the two of us were Company men in the service of our country,
and I wanted him to believe me when I held him in my arms:
we were in this together, no matter how far off I might have seemed,
I was on his side for now, for as long as it took him to make
his precarious way back to himself. Beyond that, I couldn't say.
He did most of the talking anyway, whispering his terrible secret
confusion in my ear: he wanted to die, no he didn't, and yes, please,

45

and he was going to make up his mind if it was the last thing he did
before he stepped out of that fountain hours later, dazed but renewed
or before he drew his gun like a different conclusion entirely.
The world behind his eyes was a hideous flower in bloom, and he
was going to pull off its petals, one by one, until he had his answer.

The crowd that had sprung up around us by then stood quietly,
not quite sure what they were seeing: old-fashioned slapstick or dedication
in action: two grown men in suits in a fountain, drenched and carrying on
in the line of duty, in the name of research. I wanted him to see it
my way, even for a minute, as if we had that kind of time forever
and we'd never be infiltrated again, compromised over and over
by the relentless white light of another day we really believed this time
would come over to our side after years of working against us,
spilling its colorful guts like sunlight when it hits the fountain's spray
exactly right. We wouldn't need any more coffee to keep us up all night
the rest of our lives.

        Meanwhile, the laboratory boys have who-knows-
what in mind. They're still sweating out the fate of the Free World
if only we could see them already heading back to their drawing board,
trying to keep quiet about some new plan sure to save the day tomorrow:
No one's seen anything yet. But it's no secret what's coming
through the curtains in the morning. In spite of what we thought we saw
in the day before. That's what I'm afraid of. And I could have told them so.

iii. Frank Olson Is Flying

We do not target American citizens. The nation must to a degree take it on faith that we who lead the CIA are honorable men, devoted to the nation's service.
    —Richard Helms, former CIA Director

In 1953 at the Deep Creek Lodge in western Maryland—originally built as a Boy Scout camp twenty-five years earlier—the Agency threw a get-together for its Army friends on the cutting edge of biological warfare. We don't know what kinds of stories they told around the fire, but these guys were a long way from Boy Scouts. It was going to be a harum-scarum night, and they weren't always prepared:

Frank Olson—family man, lover of practical jokes, specialist in the airborne delivery of disease—was handing out his trademark exploding cigars when the room started pinwheeling unbelievably around him. A kaleidoscope turning in his head. He'd had no more than his usual two fingers of Cointreau, so he figured it was someone's idea of fun, someone trying to kid the kingpin of kidders. He resorted to his favorite expression—*You guys are a bunch of thespians!*—his distinctive way of saying he was onto them now, the joke was over. But when a general cleared his throat and announced that certain guests had been slipped a *mind-altering chemical* as part of a *Classified experiment*, Olson wasn't laughing anymore.

It was all he could do to navigate the dark hallway back to his room. From out of his pockets he took his unused sticks of Onion Gum, his packets of Itching Powder. He unpinned his Squirting Carnation, his very own Purple Heart. He stared at his ridiculous arsenal of tricks and began a night of sobbing that wouldn't quit. He'd been caught in mid-sip with a version of the Fly-in-the-Ice-Cube, and it was too late now to spit it out. He felt like that guy in the drawing on the package, smoke and lightning coming out of his ears, his eyes popping out of his reddened cartoon face. It was hard to tell if he was angry, or embarrassed. And someone in the background, pointing and laughing. That always seemed to be an important part of the picture, too.

When Olson somehow found his frazzled way home the next day, he barely spoke with his wife, Alice: *Wait until the kids go to bed and I'll talk to you*. But all he could manage out of his own bleariness even then: *I made a terrible mistake*. She tried to tease it out of him, or at least tease him out of his malaise. When she smiled her most provocative smile and called him *Mr. Secrets*, he informed her that whoever wasn't making fun of him was trying to destroy him. And suddenly, what choice did she have? She didn't know whether to laugh or to cry.

In the weeks that followed, his anxiety grew. He only wanted to sleep, but the thought of closing his eyes made him nervous. He couldn't even make it through the simplest grace before meals. Not that he felt much like eating. A bite or two was all he could ever choke down. He was nervous going out the door, nervous in his car, nervous all day at the office where the telephone on his desk was a bomb that could go off at any time.

And if Frank Olson was nervous, the CIA was nervous. If Olson was spinning further out of control, an accident waiting to happen, they had to be more than a little concerned about the inevitable pile-up behind him. They gave him the name of a doctor with Top Secret clearance in New York who worked with LSD under Agency contract. Maybe he could bring Olson around, back to his predictable, good-natured self.

And when it was Olson's turn to sign in with the waiting-room receptionist, he couldn't help but notice the X-Ray Specs she was wearing. *What a bunch of thespians*; they'd been expecting him. He took out his most reliable pen and wrote his name in Disappearing Ink. By the time the nurse had prepared the Foot-Long Hypodermic Water Pistol, he was already gone. He'd decided: there was nothing anyone could do to change his mind.

• • • •

Frank Olson is flying, and if he ever stops
it's a long way down. He's thrown himself through
the drawn blinds, the closed window
of his tenth-floor room at the elegant Statler Hotel.
He's not thinking of terrible secrets, sweet revenge
or his footnoted place at the bottom of another page
of history. This begins his moratorium on thinking.
For weeks he's had nothing but bad ideas: poison
pen notes from his own secretary. The gas jockey's
small talk, some mockery in code. The Agency, dropping
a dime sure to lead to his imminent arrest. Everything
boiling down to the sticky, obvious residue of his undoing.

And so he'd show them all in the end
what he could still do: Frank Olson is flying high,
and if he ever stops, it won't be to reconsider
the voices that keep telling him to tear up his papers,
his money, to throw away his wallet, set fire to his clothes.
It's a long way down, and tonight the lights of 33rd Street
are burning for him: the smoke shop's got his favorite brand,
the all-night grocery if he's hungry, a tavern
where the regulars could make him feel right at home.
He's not the kind of guy to get out much, but tonight
is a different story: Frank Olson is flying
smack in the face of what will become the official
version of his dying: he will have jumped or maybe
fallen out of a window in New York because he suffered
from chronic ulcers. And it's someone else's turn

to worry now. Frank Olson is flying, and if he ever stops
someone will be working hard to make sure there's no
connection between a dead man and the CIA. Let alone
LSD. Someone will bring his widow the late-breaking news,
a bad dream in the middle of the night. And she'll wait

twenty-two years until she wakes up to what really happened,
a copy of *The Washington Post* at her door with its story
about years of illegal CIA *domestic operations*. And for her,
too, it's going to be a long way down. Finally she'll know

everything: Frank Olson—specialist in the airborne delivery
of things insidious and nearly invisible—is goddamn
flying. And if he ever stops, it's got to be
a long way down to the bottom, to the sickening thud
of a life falling apart this irretrievably. To the flashing
lights of the squad car and the spiritless chalk outline
of one more broken man on the sidewalk, all that's left
to represent him. It's crazy, what in the world
can push some people over the edge, the cop might say
to no one in particular. Certainly not to the widow Alice,
so many unsuspecting years away from the scene of the crime.

She'll have to think about it this way: her husband knew
exactly what he was doing, and he couldn't help himself.
In her better dream he's flying, no matter how desperately,
and she sees him firing up the trick cigar of his life,
right there before the lights go out. She only wishes
he could be here to watch it explode—this long after
it was handed over—in someone's fat, astonished face.
Yeah, that's real funny, Frank. I mean it this time. Funny.

Frank Olson is flying. And it's a long way down.

iv. Why It Almost Makes Sense

LSD. LBJ. FBI. CIA.
　　　　—lyric from *Hair: An American Tribal Love-Rock Musical*

Because under the cover of slapstick, the more ridiculous
the better, our spooks were willing to try anything once
so easy to laugh at, to disavow if anyone ever went public:
telepathy, REM sleep-teaching, sensory deprivation,
hypnotically induced anxieties, tunnel vision, cluster headaches,
subliminal projection, aphrodisiacs, electroshock and psycho-
suggestive lobotomy, sneezing powders, stinkbombs, exploding
cigars, marijuana, heroin, speed, diarrhetics, laughing gas.
And could someone please tell them what's so funny about LSD?

Because it was still the Cold War, it was Frostbite Falls USA
and Moose & Squirrel could cut up all they wanted—as long
as they found some way to defuse the dastardly shtick
of Boris & Natasha, *dahlink*. Because Fred MacMurray was riding
high, the Absent-Minded Professor who discovered flying rubber.
And so what's next, after his souped-up jalopy, beyond the sheer
Flubber hijinks and yucks? Because The Company's still looking
for the flimsiest practical application: maybe a little LSD
in Castro's scuba-diving mouthpiece, some itching powder in his wetsuit
would be enough to drive him crazy, cause him to go down for good.
Because no one's coloring with a full box of crayons, no one's
staying inside the lines anymore. And this is the best
they've come up with so far at the Central *Intelligence* Agency.

Because finally LSD was a whisper away from people in the street
and who knew what those unsuspecting idiots would do when it got there?
Because they were barely out of the narcotic dark of the '50s. Because
they'd dance and dance, but never give the spooks their cockeyed due:
the linguistic invention of *tripping*. Because the Agency knew, LSD
or no, the KGB demanded getting back to, the Mafia and the Kennedys
and Castro again, LBJ and maybe Elvis, Vietnam's opium highway,

another nickel's-worth of dictator to bury or embrace. Because what
the hell, acid might yet work its confusing magic to CIA advantage
if only they'd give up quietly, let it go. Because the world
wasn't about to change overnight, why not: let the damn sunshine in.

IV
THE ACCOMPLICE

THE ACCOMPLICE

This poem isn't an intricate theory years in the making.
This poem can speak only for this poem.
This poem will tell you it's not what you think.
This poem is nothing more than a series of coincidences.
This poem can't help but attract the occasional crackpot.
This poem is offered in full compliance with the Freedom of Information
   Act.
This poem is not anything like the Official Version.
This poem is holding something back.
This poem is covering up.
This poem may be afraid of worldwide panic.
This poem is no secret prototype the government is testing.

This poem has a lot of powerful friends behind it.
This poem is something you'd be happier not knowing.
This poem is murder on reliable eyewitnesses.
This poem is counting on your complete cooperation.
This poem can put you at the scene of untold crimes or
this poem is your iron-clad alibi, depending.
This poem doesn't want anything to happen to you.
This poem hopes you get the message, although
this poem has no explicit message of its own.
This poem can't promise it will bail you out.
This poem won't even remember you.
This poem is well aware of the statute of limitations.

This poem means what it says.
This poem means anything you need it to.
This poem has seen things hard to believe.
This poem is all you have to believe.
This poem has implications.
This poem couldn't possibly be.
This poem is so good it ought to be illegal.
This poem is the only hard evidence recovered.
This poem has your prints all over it.
This poem has recently been discharged.

This poem is not a disgruntled loner acting spontaneously.
This poem has been seen consorting with other known poems.
This poem has confederates in top-floor windows all over the city.
This poem never goes by the same name twice.
This poem has no highly trained Russian look-alike.
This poem never received specific instructions.
This poem has nothing better to do.
This poem can hit you where you live.
This poem seldom misses at this distance.

This poem has its story down cold.
This poem doesn't want to have to say it more than once.
This poem has never seen its share of the money.
This poem is just the patsy.
This poem laughs at the Witness Protection Program.
This poem wants immunity before it starts naming names.
This poem isn't taking the fall for anyone.
This poem has you exactly where it wants you.

This poem you think you're getting to the bottom of right now,
this poem that's taken you into its confidence,
this poem that's made you an accomplice-after-whatever-the fact,
this poem suggesting in so many words that it's always been on your side:

this poem doesn't make those kinds of mistakes.
This poem will give you up every time.

AUTHOR'S NOTE

This book—really, a kind of "Book One" of an ongoing imagined history of twentieth-century American paranoia and conspiracy theory, *Breathing in the Twentieth Century* (*conspiracy*, from the Latin *conspirare*, "to breathe together")—appropriately relies on the help of a whole lot of other folks, other writings, other information. Because there are sometimes only shades of difference between information and *mis*information, there's undoubtedly some of that here, too. And as for *dis*information—in intelligence circles, misinformation purposely delivered to achieve a certain effect—well . . . only time and security leaks will tell.

So, I would like gratefully to acknowledge my debt to:

Everyone's Uncle Bud. Stanton Friedman (with Don Berliner, *Crash at Corona*). Kevin Randle (with Donald Schmitt, *UFO Crash at Roswell*, then *The Truth About the UFO Crash at Roswell*—a revision with a telling re-titling). Jesse Marcel, Jr., who handled the debris in his childhood kitchen. Kenneth Arnold (with Ray Palmer, *The Coming of the Saucers*). *The Roswell Daily Record*. Glenn Dennis, Roswell mortician (*The Glenn Dennis Story*). Deon Crosby and the UFO Museum and Research Center, Roswell, NM. Karl Pflock (*Roswell in Perspective*). Daniel Cohen (*The Great Airship Mystery*). Jules Verne (*Robur the Conqueror*). Pulpmeister Luis Saranens, who faded into unbelievable obscurity. Edgar Rice Burroughs (*A Princess of Mars*), who didn't. Jerome Clark (for his well-researched, well-written three-volume *UFO Encyclopedia*). George Adamski (*Flying Saucers Have Landed; Inside the Space Ships*). Howard Menger (*From Outer Space to You; The High Bridge Incident*)—my personal favorite of all the '50s contactees; he and wife Connie are aces in my book. George Van Tassel (*I Rode a Flying Saucer*). Buck Nelson (*My Trip to Mars, the Moon, and Venus*). Robert Stone (for his Discovery Channel documentary about the heyday contactees, *Farewell, Good Brothers*). Robert Girard, curmudgeonly and masterful proprietor of Arcturus Books, Port St. Lucie, FL. Gabriel Green (*Let's Face the Facts About Flying Saucers*). The USAF (*Project Blue Book; The Roswell Report*). Ruth Norman and the Unarius Foundation, El Cajon, CA. J. Allen Hynek, first for 1966's laughable *swamp gas* explanation, then for the rest of his life as diligent, thoughtful investigator. George Knapp, Nevada reporter who broke the Area 51 story. Bill Morrison (creator of the *Roswell* comic book series). H.C. Hale, cheerful purveyor of Roswell crash site soil. Disney Studios' *Silly Symphonies*, particularly Buckey Bug. Richard Rhodes (for his entrancing, Pulitzer Prize–winning *The Making of the Atomic Bomb*— maybe as close to a wonderful novel as nonfiction ever gets). Ray Santilli, for buying the Alien Autopsy film footage and wheeler-dealering it to TV and video worldwide. Graham Birdsall, for his careful dissection of same (*The Alleged Roswell Archive Footage: The Definitive Report*). Elvis Presley. James Moseley, editor and still Supreme Commander (*Saucer Smear*, the liveliest eight pages to appear regularly and deflate the pompous solemnity of so much 'ufology'). Timothy Leary. The Central *Intelligence* Agency. Martin Lee & Bruce Shlain (for the indispensable *Acid Dreams: The Complete Social History of LSD*). Philip Agee (*Inside the Company: CIA Diary*). Victor Marchetti (*The CIA and the Cult of Intelligence*). John Marks (*The Search for the 'Manchurian Candidate': The CIA and Mind Control*). Warner Bros., for Tweety and Sylvester. Jay Ward, for Rocky & Bullwinkle. Aldous Huxley (*The Doors of Perception*). *The Washington Post*. Fred MacMurray, in *The Absent-Minded Professor*. Al Hidell and Joan d'Arc (editors of the engaging quarterly, *Paranoia*). Kenn Thomas (editor of *Steamshovel Press*, the zestiest—if irregular—magazine trafficking in subjects near and dear to the heart of this book). Larry, my refrigerator repairman, who's convinced that every one of us is tracked via imperceptible fibers imbedded in our paper money.

On the far side of the looking-glass, the world of alternative histories, fringe beliefs, paranoia, and conspiracies seems never explorable enough. But these sources have helped me sort out some of the ponderables, at least. We are all in on this together . . . *aren't we*?

And a huge tip of the cockeyed hat to Thomas Pynchon for *The Crying of Lot 49*, one of the first and still finest pieces of writing to take the pulse of a particularly American spirit of conspiracy and paranoia.

David Clewell is the author of six previous collections of poems, including *Blessings in Disguise* (Viking Penguin), *Lost in the Fire* (Garlic Press), and *Now We're Getting Somewhere* (U. of Wisconsin Press). He teaches writing and literature at Webster University in St. Louis.

He is not now, nor has he ever been—to the best of his knowledge—a member of the U.S. military, the executive branch of the U.S. government, the FBI, the CIA, or The Amalgamated Flying Saucer Clubs of America. Once upon a time he was briefly a member of the Raritan River Rats, a cadre of kids who communicated through a complicated network of sewer grates and drain pipes. But when the talk turned to unsavory ways of toppling world regimes and the inevitable infighting began, he walked away—toward the 3rd Avenue Sweet Shop—and never looked back.

The Conspiracy Quartet *is published in an edition of 1,000 copies, 26 of which have been lettered and signed by the author for friends of Garlic Press.*

Garlic Press
606 Rosewood
St. Louis, Missouri 63122

Peter Genovese, Editor & Publisher

Cover Art: Kevin Belford
Design: Patricia Clewell